Stephen Curry

The incredible story of Stephen Curry - one of basketball's greatest players!

Table of Contents

Introduction

Thank you for taking the time to pick up this book about the NBA champion, Stephen Curry!

This book serves as a biography of Stephen Curry, documenting his inspiring journey to the NBA, his time there, and also speculating what's next for the Champion!

In his relatively short career, Stephen Curry has been able to achieve a lot. As the son of an NBA player, Curry grew up around basketball, and soon developed a deep passion for the game!

In the following chapters you'll learn all about Stephen's first experiences with basketball, his college career, and also his incredible NBA success.

This book also discusses Curry's life outside of basketball, his family, faith, and what could be next for the exciting NBA champion.

Once again, thanks for taking the time to read this book, I hope you find it to be interesting!

Chapter 1:

Early Life

Steph Curry (full name Wardell Stephen Curry II) was born on March 14, 1988 in Akron, Ohio. His father, Dell Curry, is a former professional basketball player in the National Basketball Association. His mother, Sonya, was a former NCAA Division I volleyball player. Curry spent much of his childhood years in Charlotte, North Carolina mainly because his father was still playing for the Charlotte Hornets. For a period of time, the family also relocated to Toronto, Ontario, Canada, where Dell finished his NBA career with the Toronto Raptors.

Growing up, Steph and his younger brother Seth picked up the athletic bug from their parents quite early. Steph himself started playing basketball at the young age of five. Dell would take his two children to Hornets warm-ups before games and they would shoot around with the rest of the team. Interestingly, Steph starred in a Burger King commercial (along with his dad) when he was a child, but it seems the youngster knew he wanted to pursue basketball more than show business.

Many may think it's the athletic genes that gave Steph the basketball skills early on in life, but his father attests to his determination and love for the game even at a young age. In an interview with USA Basketball, the elder Curry relates, "He had been around it his whole life, obviously, with me playing in the NBA, so it was nothing new to him. But he started at a very young age and we just tried to make sure he got the proper skill set, the proper teaching of skills and fundamentals so that he grew and developed his game. He knew how to play and learned about the game and knew how to develop his skills and how to go about working at it."

Dell adds, "He always had good ball-handling abilities and could shoot the ball. He was always the smallest kid on every team he played, but he was one of the hardest workers... Being around NBA players really helped him because it taught him the game. He was at all the practices. He watched and learned how to play the game the right way, how to use his teammates. There was a process. Being around guys that you see are the best in the world really helps youngsters stay positive about the game. And it tells them that if they do love the game and they work at it they can reach new levels."

Steph attended Charlotte Christian School in North Carolina when his father retired from the NBA. Naturally, he became a varsity basketball player for the school, leading Charlotte Christian to three conference titles and three state playoffs. He was also named to the all-conference and all-state teams. The young Curry also showed interest in other sports, particularly football, baseball, and golf. Steph would play golf with his dad when he was around 6 years old, and was actually quite good at it.

"He was a very good baseball player, then he found golf," Dell says. "He must have hit a really good golf shot when he was playing a round with me and decided that's the way he wanted to go. He used to play golf with me when he was 6 or 7. I had a putter cut down and I'd take him with me. He'd ride in the cart, watch us play, and then when we got to the green he'd chip and putt."

Life for the Curry family was quite comfortable. Dell's salary as a Hornets player was upwards of $20 million, and they lived in a gated community in Uptown Charlotte. Home for the young Steph was a sprawling 8,305-square-foot mansion on a 16-acre property, equipped with a basketball court, pool, and hot tub. The Curry residence had six bedrooms and nine bathrooms. It was conveniently situated about four miles from their school, Charlotte Christian.

While the Curry siblings grew up quite comfortably, they did develop a strong work ethic and appreciation for hard work and determination thanks to their upbringing. They shared in the household chores, including washing dishes and giving their dogs baths. In his years of playing with Charlotte Christian, he understood very early on that he had to prove himself as a player like everybody else, despite his father's status.

Shonn Brown, one of Curry's coaches at the school, recalls in an interview with Sporting News, "If we had a 6 a.m. workout, the Currys were here. First ones in. Last ones to leave. Taking game film home and watching it as we're preparing for opponents. Every year he brought something new to his game. And that was truly just a function of him working."

One summer, Steph decided to let his father tutor him on improving his shooting form, particularly his jump shot. "It was tough for me to watch them in the backyard, late nights and a lot of hours during the day, working on the shot," Seth, Steph's younger brother, said to ESPN. "They broke it down to the point where he couldn't even shoot at all. . . . He had to do rep after rep after rep to the point where he was able to master it."

Their father agreed. "That was a tough summer for him," Dell recalled. But those long, hard days paid off as Steph soon mastered his above-the-head shot, something he would need in order to play college ball because of his size. Most of his opponents would be taller than him, even in the guard position, so if he wanted to score, he would have to find a way to make up for his lack of size.

Despite Steph being smaller in height and frame, he was able to prove himself as a capable basketball player for Charlotte Christian. He soon attracted the attention of Bob McKillop, the coach at Davidson College in North Carolina. The college showed early interest in Curry and aggressively recruited him, although the up-and-coming star originally had his sights set on playing for Virginia Tech where his father had also made a mark. The Hokies only offered Curry a walk-on spot, so he decided to play for Davidson, also an NCAA Division I school.

Coach McKillop saw potential in Steph that many overlooked. "I never thought there was a physical detriment," he says. "From the first time I saw him play on a basketball court, I thought he was going to be a star... His vision isn't just the vision of being one step ahead in terms of the action on the court. His vision is also his ability to see what's in front of him."

Both Brown and McKillop attest to Curry's high basketball I.Q. which made his teammates better at the game as well. Brown particularly goes back to Steph's junior season at Charlotte Christian where he specifically told the player to "take more shots".

The young Curry's response was, "I don't want guys thinking I'm selfish."

Coach Brown had to make it clear for him: "Let me rewind it and say it this way," Brown said. "For us to have more success, you have to take more shots."

"It was definitely not about him," Brown adds. "He is concerned about what his teammates think. He knows his first job as a point guard is to set people up. That in itself made him a better player."

This brand of unassuming leadership raised Charlotte Christian's level altogether, helping the school make the state tournament three times with Steph at the helm, as well as achieve a runner-up finish.

But McKillop also points out Steph's continuing desire for excellence that propelled him to push further and become a better player year in and year out. "He had no fear of failure," McKillop narrates. "If he missed a shot, missed five shots, he didn't care. It didn't disrupt him. It didn't destroy his focus. He knew he was going to make the next five."

Both coaches also credit much of the humility, selflessness, and confidence of Steph Curry to the parenting of Dell and Sonya. Steph is outspoken about his Christian faith, but does so without coming across as preachy or arrogant, all while living an exemplary life among those in his circle.

According to Brown, who still keeps in regular contact with Steph despite his status, "If you really know him, he would take the time. He's so giving that, I wonder, how hard is it when he has to keep walking forward?"

Chapter 1: Early Life

Coach McKillop, meanwhile, has this to say about Steph: "You find me a pro athlete today that can have that balance between humility and confidence that he has, and I'll be shocked."

Chapter 2:

College

Steph Curry originally wanted to play for the Hokies in college, just like his father. But Virginia Tech could only offer him a walk-on spot, so Curry decided to play for Davidson College, a Division I school in North Carolina competing in the Atlantic 10 Conference. Playing for the small, private liberal arts college gave Curry a chance to grow even more as a player without much hype or attention at the beginning.

That doesn't mean, of course, that the people behind the basketball program at Davidson, notably head coach Bob McKillop, were unaware of his potential. At a Davidson College alumni gathering prior to Curry's first game, McKillop told the crowd, "Wait 'til you see Steph Curry. He is something special." McKillop was one of those instrumental in recruiting Curry and convincing him to play for Davidson, and the young star did not disappoint.

Michael Cruse of *Bleacher Report* described Steph as a "a skinny, unafraid, 19-year-old kid who could end up being the most important player in the history of Davidson basketball." And Steph did just that.

Steph's first collegiate game was against Eastern Michigan, where he scored 15 points. In his next game, versus Michigan, he tallied 32 points, 4 assists, and 9 rebounds. That season, Curry led the Southern Conference (at the time, Davidson was part of this conference) in scoring, averaging 21.5 points per game. Nationally, he ranked second among freshmen in points, behind first-ranked Kevin Durant (playing for the University of Texas).

Curry led his school to the NCAA tournament, where the 13th-seed Davidson Wildcats played against Maryland. Curry led the game with 30 points, but they lost to Maryland 82-70. Still, at the end of his freshman season, Steph was named Freshman of the Year and Tournament MVP of the Southern Conference, and selected for the All-Tournament team, All-Freshman team, and First team.

After the season, Steph was selected to play for the USA team at the 2007 FIBA U19 World Championships. Once again, he showed his prowess by averaging 9.4 points, 3.8 rebounds, and 2.2 assists in 19.4 minutes. The USA national team won the silver medal in this tournament.

Steph's sophomore season with the Davidson Wildcats was even more striking. By this time, he had already grown to his adult height of 6"3. He led the Southern Conference in scoring, averaging 25.5 points per game, and also averaged 4.7 rebounds and 2.8 assists per game. Davidson finished the 2008 season with a 26-6 record and 20-0 in the conference, earning their third straight NCAA tournament appearance.

Davidson played seventh-seed Gonzaga in the NCAA tournament in 2008. Gonzaga had an 11-point lead at the start of the second half, but Curry's 30 points in the half propelled the Wildcats to a stunning 82-76 win. It was the school's first tournament win since 1969. In the second round, Davidson faced heavily-favored Georgetown (2nd seed) and the Wildcats had a deficit of as much as 17 points, but once again, Curry led the team with 25 points in the second half and Davidson upset Georgetown, 74-70.

Jason Richards, the senior point guard for the Wildcats at the time, recalls, "It was crazy. UNC played in the game after us, and all their fans were chanting for us. Steph totally won them over."

The Wildcats' next opponent was third-seeded Wisconsin, whom they defeated 73-56 behind Curry's 33 points. At that game, LeBron James of the Cleveland Cavaliers was in the stands watching, and even visited the Wildcats locker room after the game. Richards recalls, "That was incredible. When the Cavs came to Charlotte to play the Bobcats a few weeks later, the greatest player in the world—after Steph, that is!—invited all of us to be his guests."

Davidson advanced to the Elite 8 of the NCAA, setting them up against the top-seeded Kansas Jayhawks. Curry scored 25 points, including his record 159th three-pointer of the season, but the Wildcats lost to the eventual NCAA champions Jayhawks, 59-57. In this season, Steph joined Jerry Chambers, Clyde Lovelette, and Glenn Robinson as the only college players to score more than 30 points in their first four NCAA tournament games.

Again very much impressed by Steph, *Bleacher Report's* Michael Cruse wrote, "He did things to put little Davidson in the Sweet 16, and then the Elite Eight, that were unbelievable even to those of us who have been trained to just about expect the unexpected with him."

Chapter 2: College

"What Stephen became in March was the face of an increasingly elusive guilt-free fan experience. ... It wasn't that long ago, after all, that Stephen Curry was only quasi-known just around Charlotte, and then mostly as the short, scrawny son of former Hornet and overall good guy and community man Dell Curry."

Steph finished his sophomore season averaging 25.9 points, 2.9 assists, and 2.1 steals, earning him a nomination for an an ESPY in the the Breakthrough Player of the Year category. Steph was also named the Most Outstanding Player of the Midwest Region in that year's NCAA Men's Division I Basketball Championship tournament. After the 2008 season, there was some speculation that he would go professional, but Curry announced that he would be coming back to play for Davidson College as a junior.

By this time, Curry had caught the attention of many NBA scouts and avid basketball experts, and rumors were going around that he may be signing up with an NBA team especially after his stellar Elite Eight run with Davidson in his sophomore season. But Curry made it clear he wanted to stay with Davidson, and also gave credit to his teammates when asked about their team's advancing to the Elite Eight in the NCAA tournament.

"It's nothing special that I do," Curry said at that time to ESPN ahead of their Elite Eight matchup with Kansas. "I just get screens from Andrew [Lovedale] and Thomas [Sander] and other big guys down low. When I'm open, I get the ball, and I have a lot of confidence to shoot it. Nothing special that I'm doing."

He added, "It's easy to give a lot of glory to yourself when you have a lot of success. And I could get into the mindset that everything I'm doing is because of me. But I just can't think like that."

His humility and Christian faith also took center stage as his star rose in the college ranks. When asked about the Scripture quotation on his shoes, Steph remarked, "It's Philippians 4:13. 'I can do all things through Him who strengthens me.' It's always been one of my favorite Bible verses. I realize that what I do on the floor isn't a measure of my own strength. Having that there keeps me focused on the game, a constant reminder of who I'm playing for."

Early on, even as a college player, Curry knew the temptation to let it all get into his head would be there, and he had to overcome it. "It's easy to get caught up in playing for the crowd, trying to play a game you're not capable of. I found myself doing that a little bit in high school and early in my college career. I try harder not to do things that are over my head, not do anything too special. I'm more of a blue-collar guy."

His best friend at Davidson, Bryant Barr, who also played for the team, was his closest confidante and one of the reasons he was able to keep his head above water. "We have so many similarities on how we view the world, starting with our faith," Curry said about Barr in an interview. "It's been huge to have someone I can be accountable with. At any point of the day I can call Bryant and he can give me the best advice when it comes to decisions I need to make in life because he's seeing things through the same lens that I am."

The two have remained best friends to this day, even though Barr decided to pursue a career in the corporate world. "If you pointed me out to someone and said that's Steph's best friend, and they didn't know anything else about me then I could understand how they might expect me to envy Steph," says Barr.

IIe adds, "If someone sat down and got to know me they would see that I'm 100% content with where I am. I knew early on basketball wasn't going to be how I made my career. I'm loving what I do now, and I wake up on a daily basis and get to do things that give me joy and energy, and I'm happy knowing that Steph gets to do the same thing."

Returning to Davidson for his junior year, Steph averaged 28.6 points, 5.6 assists, and 2.5 steals, leading the NCAA in scoring. He scored his college career-high 44 points on November 18, 2008 in a loss to Oklahoma. Three days later, in Davidson's 97-70 win over Winthrop, Curry registered his career-high 13 assists alongside his 30 points. The Wildcats finished 18-2 in the conference and again reached the Southern Conference tournament.

Their first opponent was Appalachian State, who they defeated 84-68 again led by Curry with 43 points, the third most points in Southern Conference tournament history. However, in the semifinals, Davidson dropped their game versus the College of Charleston, 59-52. The Wildcats did not get an NCAA tournament bid, but instead were given the sixth seed in the NIT and played third-seeded North Carolina in the first round. They defeated the Gamecocks, 70-63. Curry's final college game was against the Saint Mary's Gaels in the second round of the tournament. He registered 26 points, 9 rebounds, and 5 assists in an 80-68 loss.

Steph opted out of his senior year at Davidson College, but he has said publicly that he wants to go back one day and finish his degree. "I knew what I signed up for when I went to Davidson," Curry said. "I made a promise to coach [Bob] McKillop and my family that when I left school back in '09 that that would be accomplished -- and it will be soon. Hopefully sooner than later."

He added, "It's still a priority for sure; obviously there's a lot going on right now. Taking advantage of my career right now on the court in the NBA, it's only a very short window, so you want to give all the attention and effort. But to be able to finish out that part of my life, whenever it does happen, will be huge."

Davidson College has also announced that Curry's college jersey will not be retired officially until he finishes his courses and graduates, citing a school policy that only retires the jerseys of former players who have officially graduated.

"There has not been an exemption for it, to my understanding, for anyone," Jim Murphy, athletic director for Davidson, told ESPN in 2015. "The policy itself speaks a lot to what Davidson is all about. It'd be an interesting discussion, but it hasn't been started yet."

Chapter 3:

NBA Career

Stephen Curry entered the 2009 NBA Draft, and was selected by the Golden State Warriors as the seventh overall pick. He was given a four-year, $12.7-million contract. Curry had a solid rookie year, averaging 17.5 points, 5. 9 assists and 1.9 steals for the Warriors. In that season's NBA Rookie of the Year voting, he finished second to Tyreke Evans, and was selected to the NBA All-Rookie First Team.

Describing his very first game in a piece by *GQ*, Curry wrote, "I told a bunch of reporters before the game that I thought I would be a little nervous on the court. But it felt so natural out there. There wasn't really a transition period between, say, a college game and pro game. It was just ball, tip, and I felt like I'd been playing at this level for a long time."

Though he had a decent first year in the NBA, Curry later on said he was not very happy about it. "Rookie year sucked," Curry told CSN. "It was probably at the All-Star break that we were almost eliminated from the playoffs."

He added, "It was about just trying to just establish myself as a player and figure out how I could get to that next level, get better. Success at that point was just finishing the year strong. Now I still have that mindset. But we're trying to literally win every game. We're trying to elevate ourselves to another championship level. It's fun."

Curry did improve in the 2011 season, averaging 18.6 points, 5.8 assists, and 1.5 steals for the Warriors. He led the NBA in free throw percentage with a 93.4 percent average. He was also given the NBA Sportsmanship Award, winning over Charlotte's D.J. Augustin, Chicago's Luol Deng, New Jersey's Deron Williams, Portland's LaMarcus Aldridge, and San Antonio's George Hill. The rising star also won the 2011 NBA All-Star Skills Challenge.

Also in 2011, Steph married his girlfriend of three years, Ayesha Curry. Steph and Ayesha actually met each other while they were teenagers at their church youth group. ""It's funny, our parents used to make jokes about how cute we were together, but we didn't know," Steph recalls. The two reconnected when Steph went to California for a basketball camp, where incidentally Ayesha was also residing and pursuing an acting career.

Steph reached out to her on Facebook and after a few tries, Ayesha agreed to go out with him. On their first date, she recalls picking him up in her '95 Astro van and driving to Hollywood Boulevard, where they had chai tea lattes and took pictures with Marilyn Monroe impersonators. "He was so funny and silly," she says, "the absolute opposite of what I thought he was going to be."

Eventually, Steph proposed to Ayesha in her parents' driveway. "He asked me if I knew where we were standing. It was the spot where we had our first kiss," she recounted to the Charlotte Observer. "He pulled me close and started saying all these sweet things and then dropped down on one knee. I was in a state of shock." The two would get married at the church where they both grew up, Central Church of God in Charlotte, North Carolina. The Currys have two children currently, Riley and Ryan.

Steph underwent surgery to repair torn ligaments in his right ankle during May 2011. He had previously injured his right ankle back on December 8, 2010 versus the San Antonio Spurs, and had sprained the same ankle several times during the 2010-11 season, so surgery was required. He was cleared to play for the 2011-12 season, but hurt his ankle again during a January 4, 2012 game, also against the Spurs.

His injury problems continued that season when he strained a tendon in his right foot on February 22 of that year, in a game against the Phoenix Suns. Another surgery was performed in April. He underwent rehab for many months and was given a clean bill of health for the 2012-13 season. Also that year, he signed a four-year contract extension with Golden State worth $44 million.

Because Curry was just coming back from many missed games due to injuries, the Warriors' move was met with a lot of skepticism by many basketball writers. Scott Howard-Cooper wrote on NBA.com, "This was the Warriors taking on financial risk with a player who is clearly talented, but who has also been knocked from the lineup five times the last two regular seasons, not counting similar problems in past exhibition play. He would get hurt running down court without being touched."

Grant Hughes of *FanSided* had this to say: "The Golden State Warriors shouldn't give Stephen Curry a big contract extension yet. If he wants to agree to a deal well below market rate (somewhere in the range of four years and $30 million), great! Sign him up. But if he's looking for anything approaching max money (something like five years for $45 million), forget it."

Thankfully, it proved to be a good gamble for the Warriors as Steph remained healthy and was back in playing form that season. The 2012 season also gave rise to the popularity of his tandem with fellow Warrior Klay Thompson, earning them the moniker "Splash Brothers". Curry scored a career-high 54 points versus the New York Knicks on February 27, 2013.

He also set a new NBA record for most three-pointers made in one season with 272, the last three of which he made during their last regular season game versus the Portland Trail Blazers. Then-Warriors coach Mark Jackson said about Curry's shooting, "The one thing I know about Steph Curry -- he's not afraid when the lights are brightest."

The Warriors went on to win their playoff first-round series against the Denver Nuggets, and faced the San Antonio Spurs in the second round. The Warriors lost that series in six games, but were increasingly improving as a franchise and being recognized more and more as championship contenders.

The 2013-14 NBA season saw Curry moving past Jason Richardson with the most career three-pointers made in Warriors history. Steph also made his very first All-Star appearance, and was named to the All-NBA Team, averaging 24 points and 8.5 assists for the season. In the playoffs, the sixth-seeded Warriors went up against the Los Angeles Clippers and started what has become a new rivalry in the league.

In Game 4 of the series, Curry scored 33 points, including 7 three-pointers, and led the Warriors to the 118-97 win. However, the Warriors eventually lost the tightly-contested playoff series to the Clippers in seven games. Soon after the 2013 season, the Warriors named Steve Kerr as their new head coach, and the new coach began implementing many changes to the Warrior plays, among them giving Curry more of a shooting license.

Curry was quickly becoming one of the most respected shooters in the league, particularly beyond the arc. "Curry three-pointers are like everyone else's dunks," the *Wall Street Journal* said of him. "Only his misses are surprising. To watch Stephen Curry play basketball is to witness a shooter unlike any the NBA has ever seen."

While his on-court "Splash Brothers" tandem with Thompson was earning many fans, he was also developing a very strong friendship with another Warriors teammate, Draymond Green. It has been said that Green is one of the few people on the team who has the guts to tell Steph he took a bad shot.

"I get hot at him during the game, too," Curry once said laughingly, "because, I'm like, 'I shot it for a reason, Draymond. I was pretty confident I can make it.'"

"I can say anything to him, he can say anything to me," Green said, referring to his friendship with Curry. "If I'm out there slacking, he'll tell me, 'Hey come on man, pick it up!'

Green adds, "And if he's out there slacking, I'll tell him, 'Hey, pick it up! We need you to do this! We need you to be better here!' And it's hard to do that when you don't have a relationship with someone. Human nature is like, 'How are you going to say that to me?' But when you have the relationship that we have, it makes everything so simple and easy."

In many ways, Curry and Green complement each other within the Warriors' team play - to their advantage. "It's funny, because we're alike in so many ways; but it's weird, because we're different in so many ways," Green commented.

"I think in some areas, where I may be too much, he's not enough… In areas where I may need to be a little more, he doesn't want to be. In areas where I don't want to be a little more, he wants to be. I think it just helps level us out," he added.

With the Warriors offense picking up pace, and their defense tightening up, the 2014-15 season saw the team rise to a different level altogether, behind the leadership of Curry. On February 4, 2015, in a game versus the Dallas Mavericks, Steph scored a career-high 51 points in a stunning come-from-behind win that saw Golden State battle back from a 22-point deficit. Coach Kerr could see that difficult circumstances fired up Steph even more.

"Sometimes Steph plays his best when we're down big and he just senses that he has to put the Superman cape on," Kerr said after the game. "And he's so good at it. He loves the freedom of being down and saying, `All right. I'm going to let it fly and bring us back.' And that's what he did."

Even the Mavericks' head coach Rick Carlisle was impressed with Curry's performance. "He had one of those extra-special nights. I've never seen anybody in this league hit shots like that from that distance," he acknowledged.

"If I had any kind of daylight off the pick-and-roll, I was going to shoot it," Curry said about his performance that game. "I had a good feel and a good rhythm."

Steph led the voting for the season's All-Star Game, and he also won the Three Point Contest during All-Star Weekend. April 9, 2015 saw Curry breaking his own record for most three-pointers made in a season, in a game against the Portland Trail Blazers. Curry's averages for the 2014-15 season were 23.8 points, 7.7 assists, and 2 steals per game, earning him the league's Most Valuable Player award. The Warriors won 67 games in the regular season and entered the playoffs as heavy favorites.

In the first round, top-seeded Golden State faced the eighth-seeded New Orleans Pelicans, whom they dispatched in a convincing series sweep. In the second round, the Warriors went up against the Memphis Grizzlies. Curry became the first player in NBA history to register both six three-pointers and six steals in a single game, doing it in Game 5 of the series. In their series-clinching Game 6 victory, Curry made eight three-pointers, a playoff career high.

The Warriors faced the Houston Rockets in the Western Conference Finals. This was the first playoff match-up between the two teams. The Rockets, led by James Harden and Dwight Howard, could only muster one win versus Curry's Warriors, and Golden State marched into the NBA Finals, their first franchise appearance since 1975.

"We deserve to celebrate tonight but we've still got unfinished business and it's a long time coming for the Bay Area," the Warriors' Klay Thompson said after the Rockets series, amidst the excitement of the more than 19,500 fans who flocked to the Oracle Arena to watch their home team clinch the Finals berth. Confetti fell from the rafters in celebration, and the crowd chanted "M-V-P!" for Curry.

In the much-anticipated NBA Finals series versus LeBron James and the Cleveland Cavaliers, Curry struggled in the first couple of games, particularly in Game 2 where he missed 18 of 23 field goals in a 95-93 loss.

"It didn't feel right, but there is no time to really worry about that. You've got to keep shooting and try to figure it out," Curry said of his dismal performance. "I don't expect to shoot like this. I've got to play better, find better shots and be more in a rhythm throughout the course of the game for us to really assert ourselves as a team."

James credited Matthew Delleavedova's excellent defense on Curry as the key. "It had everything to do with Delly," James said. "He kept a body on Steph. He made Steph work. He was spectacular man. Defensively, we needed everything from him. When Steph shoots the ball, you just automatically think it's going in because he shoots the ball so well. He stunned me on one in the fourth quarter when he just took an in and out dribble and raised for a three and he nailed it. And that wasn't on Delly."

He added, "Dellavedova just did a great job of just trying to make it tough on Steph. That's all you can do. You make it tough on him, you get a contest, and you live with the results. I think Delly, he did that."

Curry acknowledged that something was off with his form, but refused to let it discourage him for the rest of the series. "Shots I normally make ... I knew as soon as they left my hand that they were off," Curry admitted. "That doesn't usually happen. I mean, mechanically I don't know if there is an explanation for it. I just didn't have a rhythm and didn't find one the whole game. I'm not going to let one game kind of alter my confidence."

Eventually, Steph did find his form again, especially in Game 5 where he scored 37 points in their win versus the Cavaliers. After the game, Curry told reporters, "It was a chess match and we both have a bunch of wings and guards that can fill a lineup. They made an adjustment and tried to match our lineup. I'm sure there will be another adjustment."

In Game 6, Curry waxed hot again, scoring 25 points and dishing out 8 assists. With Warriors forward Andre Iguodala also pitching in 25 points and Draymond Green's triple-double performance (16 points, 11 rebounds, 10 assists), Golden State sealed the deal and won their first championship in over 40 years.

After the game, Steph dedicated his championship to his family, particularly his father Dell. "I'm in the family business and this is for the family."

"I'm kind of speechless," Curry added. "This is special. To be able to hold this trophy and all the hard work we've put into it this season, this is special. We're definitely a great team and a team that should go down in history as one of the best teams from top to bottom."

When asked in an interview with *Business Insider* how he prepared for the championship. Curry answered, "It starts really at the beginning of a season. How you come into the season with your mindset, your sense of focus. And every step of the way I think you learn something that makes you a better player, and all those lessons really come out when it matters the most in a championship. You obviously have your routines that you rely on, then you go out and play and have fun.

"For us in basketball, we have a seven-game series, so you have time to adjust if you need to. It's a fun experience to go through, and one that I'll remember for a long time," he added.

The Warriors started the 2015-16 regular season with an impressive 24-0 record, the best in league history. Curry continued to turn up the volume in scoring, registering 40 points in their October 27 season opener versus the New Orleans Pelicans, and another 53 points also against the Pelicans two games later. Curry had a combined 118 points in the first three games of the season, something which only Michael Jordan had previously been able to do (in the 1989-90 season).

For the first time in their careers, Steph was guarded by his brother Seth when the Warriors played the Sacramento Kings on December 28. Steph recorded his sixth triple-double of his career, with 23 points, 14 rebounds (a career high), and 10 assists, and Golden State defeated Sacramento, 122-103.

"It was a very cool moment," Steph replied when asked about being guarded by his younger brother. "I missed and he let me know about it. After that I was able to see a couple go in."

Seth, meanwhile, was all praises for his older brother. "He's done that so many times throughout the year, I don't think that's me, per se. He's going to turn it up. He's done that probably once a game, had a run like that. We tried to stop him from getting going, but it's tough. The game was going so fast at that time, that's when he's at his best."

Curry played in his third All Star appearance in the 2016 All Star Game, and also competed in the Three Point Shootout where he was defeated by Splash Brother Klay Thompson.

Heading into the All-Star Break, the Warriors had a record of 48-4, the best record in NBA history within 52 games, besting the Chicago Bulls (1995-96) and the Philadelphia 76ers (1966-67).

After the festivities, Curry continued to lead the Warriors to their best season in franchise history, scoring 51 points versus the Orlando Magic on February 25 (Warriors won 130-114), and a game-winning three-pointer (46 points total for the game) on February 27 versus the Oklahoma City Thunder with 0.6 seconds remaining in overtime. At this point, Steph also set a new record for most three-pointers in a single season, with 288; he had set the previous record.

This record did not last long, however, as Steph once again upped the ante and scored 41 points over the Orlando Magic, including 7 three-point shots to again set the record at most three-pointers made in a season at the 300 mark. It also marked the 45th straight home court win for the Warriors.

"To have protected our home court 45 straight games in the regular season, it hasn't been done in history, so that's a pretty special accomplishment," Curry remarked. "That win record is still in reach."

That win record he was referring to, of course, was the 1995-96 Chicago Bulls' 72-10 record, which the Warriors eventually surpassed on April 13, 2016 with a 125-104 win over the Memphis Grizzlies. Golden State became the first NBA team to win 73 games in one season, and Curry also became only the seventh NBA player in history to join the 50-40-90 club, with a .504 field percentage, .454 three-point average, and .908 free throw average for the regular season.

Comparing him to other recent NBA greats, FoxSports.com wrote: "Curry ended the season with the greatest true shooting percentage of a high-volume scorer in NBA history. Michael Jordan never had a true shooting percentage better than .614, and Kevin Durant posted a .635 in his MVP season two years ago — Curry, when it was all said and done, finished the year with a true shooting percentage of .669."

The website added, "There should be no doubt, Curry just posted the greatest season in NBA history, and if that doesn't land a unanimous MVP vote, it's hard to believe that any season will."

Sure enough, Curry was unanimously awarded the Most Valuable Player Award of the 2015-16 NBA season, becoming only the 11th player in NBA history to win the award back-to-back. He bested San Antonio's Kawhi Leonard, Cleveland's LeBron James, and Oklahoma City's Russell Westbrook, among other notable names. Curry was the very first unanimous MVP awardee in NBA history.

"I never really set out to change the game. I never thought that would happen in my career," Curry said as he accepted the prestigious award. "What I wanted to do was be myself... I know it inspires the next generation. You can work every day to get better."

His coach, Steve Kerr, remarked, "He wants it," coach Steve Kerr said. "There's no ulterior motive. He's constantly trying to improve with no agenda... This is incredibly improbable. But there's a reason this is happening."

When asked about the additional spotlight an MVP gets, Curry was quick to acknowledge. "They're going to have more of a spotlight, and people are going to ask questions about whoever it is. When there are legends and people that I looked up to as a player -- as a young kid, as a basketball player -- Hall of Famers and guys that talk about our team, it means that obviously we're doing something good, so we keep doing it. I take it with a grain of salt."

In the 2016 Western Conference Playoffs versus the Oklahoma City Thunder, the Warriors moved to the brink of extinction with a 1-3 series deficit. But Curry and his Splash Brother Klay Thompson rallied the Warriors to three straight wins, including the Game 7 clincher at home, to return to the NBA Finals.

"You appreciate how tough it is to get back here," Curry said. "You've got to be appreciative of this accomplishment, and look forward to getting four more wins."

The 2016 NBA Finals was a rematch between the Golden State Warriors and the Cleveland Cavaliers. The Warriors had the home-court advantage because of their regular season record of 73-9, and zoomed to an early 2-0 series lead. The Cavaliers came back in Game 3, but the Warriors took Game 4 and the Cavaliers were all but written off. Cleveland, however, battled back in convincing fashion in Games 5 and 6 to force a deciding Game 7.

This series was memorable as it featured the first time in his career that Curry was ejected from a game. The ejection happened late in Game 6, as Curry's outburst after fouling out of the game led referee Jason Phillips to throw him out.

"I've never been ejected before. It was a weird feeling," Curry said. "It was just frustration and kind of hilarious the way that the last two fouls and me blowing up kind of unfolded, some of the things that were said out there."

Coach Kerr said, "Let me be clear: We did not lose because of the officiating. They totally outplayed us and Cleveland deserved to win. But three of the six fouls (called on Curry) were incredibly inappropriate calls for anybody, much less the MVP of the league."

Game 7 of the series was in Oakland, and a very tightly-contested game. But in the final minute, the Warriors were outplayed by the Cavaliers. Curry missed a crucial three-pointer in the final minute, as Cleveland came back from the 1-3 series deficit to win, 93-89. The Cavaliers became the first NBA team to win the championship after being down 3 games to 1, and it was Cleveland's first major professional sports title in over 5 decades.

A disappointed Curry told the press afterwards, "It hurts, man. Just proud of every single guy that stepped foot on the floor for our team this year... Hopefully we'll have many more opportunities to fight for championships and be on this stage because this is what it's all about."

"I didn't do enough to help my team win," Curry added. "It will haunt me for a while."

In the current 2016-17 NBA season, the Warriors have added Kevin Durant to their lineup, and are once again dominating the Western Conference. Curry continues to set new records, including most three-pointers made in a regular season game (13 versus the New Orleans Pelicans on November 7, 2016).

On December 11, in a game versus the Minnesota Timberwolves, Curry passed Steve Nash in the NBA's list of most career three-pointers made (17th rank). Steph is now also the first NBA player in history to have at least 200 or more three-point field goals made in five consecutive seasons.

Chapter 4:

Steph Off-The-Court

Off the court, Steph spends much of his time with his wife Ayesha, and their two children, Riley (5 years old) and Ryan (2 years old). They currently reside in a mansion in Alamo, California, in the beautiful Contra Costa county. Their home has five bedrooms, ten baths, and over 10,000 square feet on the estate, which is quite a lot of room for the two kids to play in. The estate is worth about $5.8 million.

During the season, when Curry has a lot of games on the road, he tries his best to stay connected to his family through technology.

"FaceTime helps me a lot," he said to Parents Magazine. "I feel like I'm at home even though I'm not...Riley is at the age where she asks where I am and when I'll be back, counting down how many "sleeps" until Daddy gets home."

Their daughter Riley became a worldwide celebrity during a 2015 press conference when she interrupted her father's interview and stole the spotlight.

"I have to walk past the family waiting room to get to the interview room, and Riley wanted to hang out with me. She had that look, like she wasn't going to take no for an answer.

So I said, all right, come with me. She sat up there, and that's when her personality shined bright," Steph recalls.

"I tried my best to answer the questions even while feeling under the table and checking out of the corner of my eye—where is Riley? She's got a great sense of humor. Now she's the star of the family. If we go somewhere without her, the first question people ask us is, 'Where's Riley?'"

In her blog, Ayesha writes a lot about their experiences in parenting. About the viral press conference with Riley, she wrote, "Stephen attends practice every day, and gives his all during the games on an almost-nightly basis. When that's over, all he wants is to see his family, and on the day of that press conference, our daughter wanted to be with her father. I thought it was beautiful for him not to push his daddy duties to the bottom of the list just because all eyes were on him. I believe you should let your children be children, and don't be afraid to be a parent, regardless of who's watching."

She adds, "Family matters! Our children matter! At the end of the day, when all the lights dim, and the cameras are gone, we are still here as his biggest, loudest, and most supportive cheerleaders. We are also extremely proud that in spite of some criticism, Riley was able to share in that experience with her father and bring joy and laughter into the lives and homes of many all over the world."

When asked by Parents Magazine how Steph is as a father, Ayesha replied, "The thing I love about him is that he's not too cool for school. He'll get down on the floor and play with the girls. He'll put on dress-up clothes if he has to, and he's very patient, which is something I'm not. We balance each other out."

Curry looks forward to seeing his kids grow up. "I think about the milestones from my childhood and what it will be like to watch our kids go through them. Taking Riley to her first day of school was a whirlwind. I can't imagine what middle school is going to be like, and high school, and graduation. All those little checkpoints are going to be fun, and there will be ups and downs along the way. Watching our children go through those life experiences will be amazing."

A central part of the Curry family experience is their Christian faith. As Steph and Ayesha both grew up in church and met in a church youth group, it was all but inevitable that their faith would also become a big part of their endeavors. In a piece for FCA Magazine, Curry recalled his childhood growing up in a Christian environment and how it shaped him to be the individual he is today.

"I remember it like it was yesterday, the day I gave my life to Christ. I was in fourth grade, and I recall hearing and understanding the gospel of Jesus Christ and walking down the aisle to give my life to Him. My parents continued to pour into my faith from that point on, making sure I understood the commitment I'd just made. Starting in middle school I attended Charlotte Christian School, which allowed me to hear the gospel on a daily basis. Looking back, my childhood was filled with the Lord's presence."

He writes further, "Fast-forward to now, and my faith continues to be my driving force. God's blessed me with an awesome support system in Oakland. We have about 10 guys on our team who attend our pregame chapels and pray together before games. The Holy Spirit is moving through our locker room in a way I've never experienced before. It's allowing us to reach a lot of people, and personally I am just trying to use this stage to share how God has been a blessing to my life and how He can be the same in everyone else's.

Despite his many successes, Curry is always quick to emphasize that it is all for something greater. "God's given me talents to play basketball for a living, but I still have to work hard to improve every day. I know that in the grand scheme of things, this is just a game that can be taken from me at any moment. But I love that basketball gives me the opportunities to do good things for people and to point them towards the Man who died for our sins on the cross. I know I have a place in heaven waiting for me because of Him, and that's something no earthly prize or trophy could ever top."

He adds, "There's more to me than just this jersey I wear, and that's Christ living inside of me."

Sure enough, there's more to Steph than just the basketball superstar that millions look up to. He is a philanthropist who generously supports several charitable causes, including NBA Cares, Animal Rescue Foundation, Nothing But Nets, and the United Nations Foundation. In particular, Nothing But Nets works closely with various UN partners across Africa to support and protect populations at risk of the deadly disease, malaria. On several occasions, Steph has publicly raised awareness regarding this organization.

Sports journalist Rick Reilly, one of the co-founders of the Nothing But Nets campaign, describes Curry as very involved with the program, especially when they went to Tanzania together to hang the malaria nets in refugee homes.

"We went to Tanzania three years ago to help Nothing But Nets deliver tens of thousands of nets," Reilly recounted. "I've never witnessed a more humble and caring athlete dedicate so much time to families."

"I was introduced to the cause in college, as well," Curry said regarding Nothing But Nets. "There was an event that Barr (his best friend) ran, a three-on-three to raise money to fight malaria. So, when Nothing But Nets approached me, it made perfect sense. Knowing the stats around malaria, how many children are affected by the disease. I have two daughters myself, and I know the feeling of wanting to protect them."

In previous years, Steph and his entire family have also partnered with the Warriors Community Foundation and Feed The Children in distributing food and other personal items to Oakland-area families in need.

"Our family has been involved with Feed The Children for many years because it is a great way to impact the lives of so many people who are desperate for assistance at this time of the year," his mother Sonya Curry said.

Pastor Charley Hames, Jr of Beebe Memorial Cathedral, a church in which many of the recipients are congregation members, said, "What Stephen and the Golden State Warriors are sharing with them is not just some food and items to ease their burden, but a reminder that there are fellow members of their community that care for their well-being ..."

For his part, Steph says, "I've been a member of [the Oakland] community since 2009, and it's important for me to give back ... to the fans that give so much to us all year long."

Chapter 4: Steph Off-The-Court

In 2015, Steph presented the 2016 Kia Sorento he was awarded as Kia NBA Most Valuable Player to the East Oakland Youth Development Center. The vehicle is being used for the center's various field trips and programs revolving around art, careers, wellness, education, and other worthy causes. The following year, when Steph won the MVP award again along with a 217 Sorento, he donated the vehicle to Covenant House, a charity for homeless youth.

"The Warriors have done a great job of reaching out to Covenant House all year long. This is kind of like the cherry on top of what basketball can bring to the community," Curry said.

In these and many other cases, Steph has given back to his community and beyond, showing his faith in action and proving that he is worthy of the emulation of today's youth.

Chapter 5:

The Future of Steph Curry

There is no doubt that Stephen Curry is at the prime of his basketball career, and is poised to improve even more facets of his game. In a piece for ESPN.com, basketball writer Benjamin Morris described Curry as the "revolution", using the player's shooting statistics over the years to postulate that indeed, Steph is more than just the hype. According to Morris, "Curry has taken on additional shot-making responsibilities throughout his career, yet his true shooting percentage has been getting better and better."

He writes further, "As I mentioned earlier, for most players, this is a trade-off: The larger the burden placed on them, the less efficient they are. I've added a trend line through all of the players other than Curry to show how it's normally flat. This is because better players tend to get more shots, which counteracts the fact that a given player taking more shots tends to be less efficient. I've also colored in LeBron James and Durant, so you can see that the standard relationship basically holds even for MVPs. But Curry has set career highs in both attempts and efficiency — in the same year — four times, including each of the past three seasons. That is, Curry comes only in shades of good, better and best (in that order). Curry is truly the Dennis Rodman of shooting!"

Chapter 5: The Future of Steph Curry

Morris says while we have already seen so much of what Curry can do, we probably haven't even seen his full potential just yet. "I don't know. But Curry himself is a microcosm of the revolution that we've already seen. Just as the math suggests that good midrange jump shots should often be exchanged for worse 3-pointers if possible, so the math suggests that good non-Curry shots should be exchanged for worse Curry shots. I'm confident in saying that we aren't there yet. And if that revolution happens as well, look out."

For now, however, the Warriors star is focused on winning more championships with Golden State. When asked about his impending free agency status after his four-year $44-million contract with the Warriors expires this season, Curry replied, "Like I've said from Day 1 when I was first asked about free agency, this is a perfect place to play. Bay Area fans are amazing, our organization's amazing, we've put together an amazing team that's competing for championships every year. There's really no reason that I can see right now that would draw me elsewhere."

It is indeed strange that despite his back-to-back MVP awards and helping the Warriors franchise win an NBA championship, Steph is only fourth in his own team in annual salary. But more than likely, the Warriors will give Curry a sizable increase in his salary and keep him in their stable, if they know what's good for them. Curry seems to want to stay in the Bay Area as well.

"It's hard to see myself anywhere else," he declared.

An article on the *Bleacher Report* indicates that while many other NBA teams who may be interested in signing Curry can offer him up to $133 million over the next four years, the Warriors can max out his contract at a whopping $209 million over 5 years. This, plus the very real possibility of a long-term playing relationship with fellow superstar Kevin Durant, might be enough to keep Curry from setting his sights elsewhere.

Curry likes the prospect of an immediate future with Durant in Golden State also. "I think he really enjoys playing with us as a team. He enjoys living in the Bay Area, the opportunities that are out here. I think he just genuinely enjoys coming to work every day. That's a good recipe for hopefully a long-term presence in the Bay."

Basketball fans and experts alike are watching Curry closely and noting that he is changing the style of basketball for a whole new generation. Andy Borman, coach of the EYBL's New York Rens, says, "The thing with Steph is he's an artist," Borman said. "The thing that he's influencing isn't really jump shooting, it's creativity and flair. For these kids, it's not about just making the simple play anymore. It's about making the beautiful play. And that's not a bad thing as long as you can do both."

Former Warriors head coach Mark Jackson didn't seem to think so, however. He famously quipped during a game commentary that Curry may not be helping the game. "Steph Curry's great. Steph Curry's the MVP. He's a champion. Understand what I'm saying when I say this. To a degree, he's hurting the game. And what I mean by that is that I go into these high school gyms, I watch these kids, and the first thing they do is they run to the 3-point line. You are not Steph Curry. Work on the other aspects of the game. People think that he's just a knock-down shooter."

Borman disagrees. "I think anyone who inspires positive feelings and a passion for the game is a good role model. That's not destroying the game, that's helping the game."

Chapter 5: The Future of Steph Curry

Curry's teammate Draymond Green was quick to come to his best friend's defense. "It's good for kids to think they can be Steph because it gives them realistic hope," he remarked.

But B.J. Johnson, assistant director of USA Basketball, reminds up-and-coming players that Curry got to where he is now, and continues to elevate his level, because of hard work and the constant desire to raise his personal standard of excellence. And West Virginia head coach Bob Huggins doesn't have a problem with Curry's influence either, because it challenges players to raise their own level of play as well.

"Curry has changed the game," Huggins said. "He's forcing new options and new opportunities. Some of the guys from the old guard who played in the '60s and '70s may not like it, but it's what keeps the game exciting. I see no problem with it."

Conclusion

Thanks again for taking the time to read this book!

You should now have a good understanding of Stephen Curry and his inspiring story!

If you enjoyed this book, please take the time to leave me a review on Amazon. I appreciate your honest feedback, and it really helps me to continue producing high quality books.

www.ingramcontent.com/pod-product-compliance
Lightning Source LLC
Chambersburg PA
CBHW051739050726
47598CB00003B/1261